白眉派

Pak Mei Kung Fu

Southern Style Staff

大陣棍

Pak Mei Kung Fu Southern Style Staff

白眉派　大陣棍

紐約白眉拳術文化保會
NEW YORK CITY

Williy Pang

TNP Multimedia LLC

Pak Mei Kung Fu: Southern Style Staff

∞

TNP Multimedia LLC
P.O. Box 130197
New York, NY 10013

Book Design by Mary Chiu.

Disclaimer:
The author, assistants, and publisher of this work and material are NOT RESPONSIBLE in any manner whatsoever for any injury which may occur through reading or following the material and/or instructions in this work.
The material and activities, physical or otherwise, described in this work may be too strenuous or dangerous for some people, and the reader(s) should consult a physician before engaging in them.

ISBN 978-0-9814813-1-9

First Edition

Printed in the United States of America

To my Family,
Without you, I would be nothing.

A NOTE ABOUT ROMANIZATION

The English equivalent of Chinese names and terms is quite often confusing due to the various dialects which are prevalent throughout China in conjunction with the occasional non-standardized Romanization of such names and terms in written form.

With the exception of the name *Pak Mei* and some proper names which have been preserved in their Wade-Giles translations (such as *Shaolin*) or other conventions to maintain their established methods of expression, the Chinese names and terms in this book will utilize a modified version of the Yale system of Cantonese to facilitate a close approximation to what the terms should sound like when enunciated in the Cantonese dialect. In this modification, the letter "h" will not be used as a tone indicator as it has been established in the Yale system.

Some terms, such as Shaolin, will be kept in their Pinyin format since they are the most familiar conventions in which most readers are accustomed to seeing.

It should be noted that the official Yale system's Cantonese written standard of the name Pak Mei is actually *Baahk Meih*.

INTRODUCTION

Pak Mei Kung Fu is a classical Chinese martial art that was refined and organized into a system of self-defense by Master Cheung Lai Chuen at the start of the 20th Century in Guangdong, China. The precursor to this text, <u>Pak Mei Kung Fu: The Myth & The Martial Art</u> by S. L. Fung, thoroughly covers the historical setting and social context of this Kung Fu system.

Translated as White Eyebrow Kung Fu – named after a famed itinerant pugilist in Southern Chinese martial folklore, the system's primary emphasis on striking skills is facilitated through sophisticated hand techniques and suppressive leg maneuvers. By effectively manipulating and attacking the limbs of the body, an assailant will be left vulnerable to visceral and cranial harm. This overall theme is evident throughout the system's unarmed techniques and use of traditional Chinese weaponry.

~

When I first considered learning Pak Mei Kung Fu in 1990, I realized that it was not going to be an easy task. First, there were very few people who even knew about it except for its cinematic portrayal via the Shaw Brothers; then, there were even fewer who actually taught it. There was no Internet, World Wide Web, Google, YouTube, or even e-mail. With Pak Mei Kung Fu, everything seemed to be by word of mouth or by way of introductions. Needless to say, I did not begin learning that year.

Sometime later, a little over two years later when my initial enthusiasm had dwindled to little more than embers of a former burning desire, I found my way to Sifu Kwong Man Fong in Sunset Park, Brooklyn, New York, just a mere neighborhood away from where I lived – the irony of it all.

The training under our teacher in Pak Mei Kung Fu was about 30% physical and 70% mental. Without the mental, you couldn't get the physical. It was about learning alignment, relaxation, and force production within every movement; and, it was about unlearning the bad habits that we had internalized throughout our entire lives like poor posture, tensional accumulation, and muscular dependence. Peter Pena, my training brother, and I took copious and detailed notes during our training and continue to do so to date. At the time, the information from our teacher came rather spontaneously and somewhat randomly when he would get "on a roll." Personal anecdotes would get mixed in with technical theory and details – the meat of the material, which would snowball into the myriad of permutations that can arise from a single technique. Then, there were the "dry spells" of stares and silences that left us wondering if we had done something wrong or had somehow inadvertently offended him. The teachings that we eventually amassed from our teacher did not come from one particular extended sitting during *yam cha* – literally to drink tea; used to express a shared dining experience typically synonymous with the more common term *dim sum*. Rather, it took endless hours of training, years of *yam cha*, and a constant referral to our notes to reinforce his prior teachings so that we could raise our understandings to the next level. We realized early on that without the principles and theories to the system, our training fell somewhere between sheer natural ability and guesswork.

Over time, with all things in perspective, we learned to refine ourselves – which is the very essence of Kung Fu.

And this leads us to this point – this text. Meant to be informative rather than instructional, this work presents many of the different aspects related to the learning and training of Daai Jan Gwan (大陣棍), or Great Formation Pole, a pillar weapon set in Pak Mei Kung Fu. While the maneuvers of this routine fundamentally manifest the essence of Southern Chinese martial arts systems: powerful, direct, and diverse, it is the principles and practice that make the techniques uniquely Pak Mei. Acquired by way of *hard work* in every sense of the phrase, those distinct ideas established both the framework and foundation of this book.

It is my sincerest hope that the knowledge shared here will provide readers with a greater understanding of Pak Mei Kung Fu, and, more importantly, reinforce their reverence for the timeless ingenuity and sophistication of traditional Chinese martial arts.

Train hard. Be well.

Respectfully,

Williy Pang

July 2010

TABLE OF CONTENTS

TABLE OF CONTENTS

CHAPTER ONE

The History

of the

Chinese Fighting Staff

"Speak softly and carry a big stick."
– Theodore Roosevelt,
26th U.S. President (1858-1919)

The staff is a revered weapon within Pak Mei Kung Fu. Its importance is even immortalized within a verse in the system's code of conduct: After you have mastered Pak Mei's fist and staff methods, you have attained a high level of achievement – not only in martial arts, but in life.

Daai Jan Gwan (大陣棍), or the Great Formation Staff, is a key staff routine trained within Pak Mei. Its origins, methods, and usage are best presented following a synopsis of the gwan (棍), or staff, in Chinese martial arts.

Note: The names of individuals in this section will be introduced in their Yale Romanization for their Cantonese pronunciations followed by their respective Pinyin format in parentheses.

Origins of the Staff in Chinese Martial Arts

In ancient China, the cheung (槍), or spear, was considered "The King of Long Weapons." With a tip initially constructed of stone, then bronze, followed by reinforced steel – the respective technologies of the times, the spear was respected for its long-range access and lethal execution. Typically wielded by military soldiers, the spear was employed by both infantry and cavalry units. These organized foot soldiers and experienced horsemen were usually found in the northern regions guarding the emperor and the capital – the head and the heart of the Chinese empire.

While effective staff skills and methods may have existed concurrently with the spear, the reputation of the staff was purportedly established by the legendary 13 Shaolin monks who deftly employed their pole methods to aid Lei Sai Man (李世民; Li Shi Min), or Taai Jung (太宗; Taizong), in his victorious campaign toward becoming the second emperor of the Tang Dynasty. The impact that this event made in the martial world was tremendous. The idea that the techniques of a mere pole

2

could compete with, and even defeat, edged weapons was unusual and astonishing. Its unassuming yet lethal potential made it a very practical weapon among civilians and unassuming individuals. As a result, many formalized pole techniques and staff skills were derived from the inspiration of this incident.

The earliest organized staff routines in Chinese martial arts were typically named after individuals who were well known for their martial expertise. According to legend, ancient staff methods were formulated and formalized into a standardized routine by Jiu Hong Yan (趙匡胤; Zhao Kuangyin) – The First Emperor of the Song Dynasty (宋朝; 960 – 1279 CE). Known as Taai Jou Gwan (太祖棍; Taizu Gun), or great ancestor staff, the techniques assembled in this routine were modeled primarily after the techniques of the spear due to similarities in both their form and execution. Taizu, as the first Song emperor is widely known by in the Mandarin dialect, is also known for devising the foundation for Long Fist (太祖長拳) – a well known Northern-based system of Chinese martial arts.

In other instances, the noted individuals were popular fictional characters rather than actual historical figures. Mou Chung (武松; Wu Song), a heroic figure of the Water Margin Classic – Seui Wu (水滸; Shui Hu; circa mid-1500s) was the inspiration for the techniques of the Traveler's Stick (行者棒), or Hang Je Paang. Considered one of the Four Canons of Classical Chinese Literary Novels, The Water Margin Classic – also known as Outlaws of the Marsh, chronicles the plight of 108 fugitives during the early part of the 12th Century in China. Within the novel, Mou Chung – widely known in

Mandarin as Wu Song, was recognized for his powerful stature and uncompromising sense of justice. He was said to have killed a tiger with his bare hands and avenged his brother's murder by killing his sister-in-law and her lover who were responsible for his brother's lethal poisoning. Wu Song's martial might and unrelenting righteousness were believed to be channeled through the fighting methods of the Traveler's Stick.

A second Traveler's Staff was named after the Monkey King, Syun Ng Hung (孫悟空; Sun Wukong), of another classic novel: Journey to the West (西遊記; circa 1590). On a side note, the remaining two classics of the Chinese literary canon are Romance of the Three Kingdoms (三國演義) and Dream of the Red Chamber (紅樓夢). The account of the mischievous Monkey King, who is often too smart for his own good, initiates the chronicles leading to the mission of monk Yun Jong (玄奘; Xuanzang; in English, he is often known as Tripitaka) whose *Journey to the West* to retrieve sacred Buddhist scriptures is accompanied by: The Monkey King, The Pig Being (豬八戒), and The Sand Creature (沙悟淨). Sun Wukong, as he is better known in Pinyin, employed a magical staff in which he could shrink to the size of a pin to fit in his ear or extend to the height of the heavens. Hence, Sun the Traveler's Staff – also known as The Monkey King's Staff, or Syun Hang Je (孫行者; Sun Xingzhe), was meant to invoke the idea of supremacy and invincibility over one's enemies in combat.

Major Staff Routines in Chinese Martial Arts

The previously described key staff routines in their respective Mandarin pronunciations: Taizu, Wu Song, and Sun Wukong, served as the ancient archetypes for the methods and techniques that are found in many staff routines to date. In subsequent staff sets passed down through families, styles, and systems, countless practitioners adopted similar methods of naming their pole routines. Individuals, clans, cultural references, martial principles, and metaphysical concepts were all manners in which practitioners distinguished staff forms from each another. The following roll is a comprehensive listing of major staff forms that have been mentioned as established routines in numerous Chinese martial arts. The Chinese characters for the staff routine's name are presented first, followed by the Cantonese pronunciation, the Mandarin pronunciation, and English translation.

羅漢棍	Lo Hon Gwan; Lohan Gun; Buddhist Arhat Pole
少林棍	Siu Lam Gwan; Shaolin Gun; Shaolin Pole
五郎八卦棍	Ng Long Bat Gwa Gwan; Wu Lang Bagua Gun; 5th Youth 8 Diagram Pole
五行棍	Ng Hang Gwan; Wu Xing Gun; Five Element Pole
六點半棍	Luk Dim Bun Gwan; Liu Dian Ban Gun; 6.5 Point Pole
八封棍	Baat Fung Gwan; Ba Feng Gun; Eight Measure Pole

六合棍	Luk Hap Gwan; Liu He Gun; Six Harmony Pole
四象棍	Sei Jeung Gwan; Si Xiang Gun; Four Form Pole
乾天棍	Gon Tin Gwan; Gan Tian Gun; Heavenly Pole
降龍棍	Gong Lung Gwan; Jiang Long Gun; Subduing Dragon Pole
八卦棍	Baat Gwa Gwan; Bagua Gun; 8 Diagram Pole
伏虎棍	Fuk Fu Gwan; Fu Hu Gwan; Subduing the Tiger Pole
降魔棍	Gong Mo Gwan; Jiang Mo Gun; Subduing Demon Pole
瘋魔棍	Fung Mo Gwan; Feng Mo Gun; Mad Devil's Pole
陳家棍	Chan Ga Gwan; Chen Jia Gun; Chan Family Pole
黑虎棍	Haak Fu Gwan; Hei Hu Gun; Black Tiger Pole
游龍棍	Yau Lung Gwan; You Long Gun; Swimming Dragon Pole
五虎棍	Ng Fu Gwan; Wu Hu Gun; Five Tigers Pole
玄武棍	Yun Mou Gwan; Xuan Wu Gun; Yun Mou Pole
文武棍	Man Mou Gwan; Wen Wu Gun; Scholar Warrior Pole

6

太極棍	Taai Gik Gwan; Tai Ji Gun; Extreme Ultimate Pole
無極棍	Mou Gik Gwan; Wu Ji Gun; Non-Polarity Pole
群羊棍	Kwan Yeung Gwan; Qun Yang Gun; Shepherd's Pole
欄門棍	Laan Mun Gwan; Lan Men Gun; Blocking the Door Pole
梅花棍	Mui Fa Gwan; Mei Hua Gun; Plum Blossom Pole
金剛棍	Gam Gong Gwan; Jin Gan Gun; Buddha Warrior's Attendant Pole/Diamond Pole
龍門棍	Lung Mun Gwan; Long Men Gun; Dragon Gate Pole
五龍棍	Ng Lung Gwan; Wu Long Gun; Five Dragons Pole
蟠龍棍	Pun Lung Gwan; Pan Long Gun; Coiling Dragon Pole
混元棍	Wan Yun Gwan; Hun Yuan Gun; Synthetic Pole
青龍棍	Ching Lung Gwan; Qing Long Gun; Green Dragon Pole
天罡棍	Tin Gong Gwan; Tian Gang Gun; Heavenly Stars Pole
飛龍虎棍	Fei Lung Fu Gwan; Fei Long Hu Gun; Flying Dragon Tiger Pole
劉家棍	Lau Ga Gwan; Liu Jia Gun; Lau Family Pole

流水棍	Lau Seui Gwan; Liu Shui Gun; Flowing Water Pole
龍形棍	Lung Ying Gwan; Long Xing Gun; Dragon Shape Pole
漁翁棍	Yu Yung Gwan; Yu Weng Gun; Fishing Old-Man's Pole
八仙棍	Baat Sin Gwan; Ba Xian Gun; Eight Immortals Pole
七星棍	Chat Sing Gwan; Qi Xing Gun; Seven Stars Pole
四門棍	Sei Mun Gwan; Si Men Gun; Four Gates Pole
空門棍	Hung Mun Gwan; Kong Men Gun; Empty Gate Pole
朱雀棍	Jyu Jeuk Gwan; Zhu Qiao Gun; Vermillion Sparrow Pole
流星棍	Lau Sing Gwan; Liu Xing Gun; Shooting Star Pole
水火棍	Seui Fo Gwan; Shui Huo Gun; Water-Fire Pole

Although this was an extensive list, it is still limited due to the lack of access to countless routines whose lineages prohibit public disclosure or have simply become extinct.

Northern Spear, Southern Staff

As previously mentioned, formalized staff techniques were initially modeled after established spear methods that were employed primarily by military troops. On the battlefield and during training in open terrain, the spear could be wielded in wide arcs to cover long distances and broader striking ranges. Agile footwork was combined with sophisticated spear skills to penetrate an opponent's weaknesses and to quickly evade overwhelming attacks. In the open expanse of the northern landscape, such techniques could be executed in this manner. Hence, early staff methods mimicked the elongated maneuvers of the spear.

In order to accommodate the conditions found in the southern regions, staff methods were altered to address stability, structural integrity, and proximity. In the southern and southeastern sections of China, the terrain is predominantly hilly with the exception of the Pearl River Delta region where the land is rather level relative to the rest of the southern countryside. The uneven surfaces required individuals to forgo mobility and to focus on a firm foundation upon which the staff could be effectively manipulated. Without the proper rooting, staff strikes would lack the appropriate force to make the techniques effective. Stable stances preserved the practitioner's foundation by anchoring the legs so that the upper body could execute techniques without fear of losing one's balance in battle. This transition from mobility to stability also affected the reach and range of functional techniques. Staff sets originating from the northern regions tended to employ daan tau (單頭), or single-ended methods, whereby the practitioner's grip was at one extreme end of the pole and the tip of the staff was used to execute the majority of the techniques – in the same manner that a spear would be wielded. Southern staff methods tended to also emphasize seung tau (雙頭), or double-ended techniques, in conjunction with single-ended maneuvers. This enabled a practitioner to take advantage of the substantial force that could be generated upward from the solid southern stances. Holding the staff at body's width from the center of the shaft strengthens close-range strikes and supports quick recovery and follow-up techniques. While the striking range may be reduced, the opportunities to feint and counter quickly are broadened with the availability of two striking ends. The counterattack from a double-ended pole can be quite unpredictable and overwhelming since there are two tips to strike with rather than one.

Spear and staff distinctions are also characterized by the positioning of the hands on the shaft of each respective weapon. The lead hand is the grip positioned toward the center of the shaft and the rear hand controls the butt end of the weapon. In most Chinese militaristic spear methods, the left hand is the lead hand and the right hand manages the base of the weapon. On the battlefield, the right hand acted as a counterweight since it was typically the one favored to perform most tasks. Dexterity and strength from sheer usage provided the grounds for it to be the more suitable candidate to control the end opposite the weighted tip of the spear. While the right hand dictated the degree of discharging force, the lead hand defined the spear's direction. In ancient combat, the synchronized actions of both hands in unison with a fully integrated physique and spirited mindset determined the warrior's survival and sealed the fighter's fate. In contrast, the staff did not have the load of a spearhead to necessitate a right-handed counterbalance at the rear of the shaft. The absence of the weighted tip enabled the staff to be wielded with the favored hand, typically the right hand, as the lead grip on the staff. This provided greater control and manipulation due to the ease with which techniques could be naturally executed with the right hand. The left grip at the rear supported the actions led by the right hand's placement. The fluency with which the staff could be manipulated in this manner made the right-lead-left-rear hand placement the preferred position for most pole methods.

Exceptions to such conventional approaches are prevalent throughout Chinese martial arts. Jau Ga Ying Cheung (周家纓槍) – Jow or Chow Family Tassel Spear, employs a right-handed lead when performing spear techniques, emphasizing the strength of both arms in wielding the spear rather than requiring the use of a right-handed counterweight to balance the weight of the spear's tip. Likewise, Hung Fut Fung Mo Gwan (洪佛瘋魔棍) – Hung Fut Style's Mad Devil's Pole, emphasizes a left-handed lead in the execution of its staff techniques. This uncommon manner of manipulating the staff can confound opponents and tends to favor the left-handed fighter. Such innovations exemplify the complexity and ingenuity of Chinese martial arts.

Weaponry within Pak Mei Kung Fu

Within Pak Mei Kung Fu, bing hei (兵器), or weaponry, is viewed as the extension of an individual's ability to manifest force from a fully coordinated and integrated body both into and throughout an object – in this case, a staff. It is believed that if a practitioner cannot issue force properly, the weapon that is wielded by the practitioner will not be able to be used effectively. Weapons in this circumstance provide the means to challenge a practitioner to meet a martial standard and to raise the practitioner's level of training and experience.

The collection of weaponry that is trained in Pak Mei Kung Fu has predominantly been imported from Lau Man Ga (流民家) – the Wanderers Sect, and Lei Ga (李家; pronounced Li in Pinyin) – the fighting methods of the Li Family. The Wanderers Sect was known to amass an assortment of weapons that ranged from established to uncommon armaments such as the double broadswords to the tiger fork, respectively. Lei Ga, on the other hand, was renowned primarily for the system's staff skills. While many practitioners have chosen to augment the system by supplementing the training curriculum with their own weapons experiences, a core set of key staff routines were deemed worthwhile to the system by Master Cheung Lai Chuen.

Lei Ga: The Source of Staff Skills in Pak Mei Kung Fu

In his youth, Cheung Lai Chuen studied under the local martial master, Lei Mung (李矇) whose acclaimed lineage stemmed from his father, Lei Yi (李義). It is important to note that there are many Lei, or Li, lineages in Chinese martial arts due to the prevalence of the surname. The Lei family name in this instance bears no relation to the Lei lineages pertaining to other martial styles such as the *Lei* Ga of Guangdong province. In this context, the fighting methods of the Lei Family were indigenous to the Dunggong region.

Recognized for its superior staff skills, Lei Ga pole techniques were highly sought after within the region. Drills consisting of reinforcement routines, comprehensive sets emphasizing staff skills, training methods addressing pole proficiency, and paired practice focusing on sensitivity and striking accuracy were all essential in the development a highly skilled exponent of the staff. Within the Lei family style, a multitude of staff methods existed to contend with all confrontations and combative situations. Of all the routines, Fuk Seh Gwan (伏蛇棍; Hidden Snake Pole), Daai Jan Gwan, and Ng Hang Jung Lan Gwan (五行中攔棍; Five Element Central Guarding Pole) were the most notable for their specialized techniques. Fuk Seh Gwan focused on stealthy techniques involving double-ended strikes in conjunction with unpredictable single-ended thrusts. Daai Jan Gwan was designed to defeat multiple attackers while Ng Hang Jung Lan Gwan taught the practitioner the finer aspects of range, redirection, and reinforcing forces within the intricate maneuvers of this particular staff form. In each routine, distinct theories and principles are trained for all situations. For these reasons, Cheung Lai Chuen chose to implement these key routines within his martial syllabus.

Peter Pena performing fei san waan gwan.

CHAPTER TWO

Daai Jan Gwan:

Foundation & Force Production

"The loftier the building,

the deeper must the foundation be laid."

– Thomas à Kempis,

Renaissance monk & author (1380-1471)

Daai Jan Gwan literally translates to Great Formation Pole, addressing the manner in which a multitude of opponents can be overcome with the aid of the techniques from this particular form. This routine emphasizes both daan tau and seung tau methods – single-ended intensified strikes in combination with double-ended versatile attacks, respectively. The effectiveness of each technique is dependent upon the intimate relationship between the practitioner and the pole – internal intent leading to external expression. In order to appropriately address the intricacies of the staff, the properties of the body must first be identified and understood within the framework of Pak Mei principles.

Foundation and Footwork

The Pak Mei ma (白眉馬), literally the Pak Mei horse, is the name of the primary stance that Pak Mei practitioners use. The poetic phrase ding bat ding, baat bat baat (丁不丁, 八不八) – [the Chinese character for] person, not person; [the Chinese character for] eight, not eight, depicts the positioning of the feet which will support the Pak Mei stance, one that is a hybrid between a pigeon-toed stance where both feet are angled inward along the same latitude and the classical bow stance where the width of the foundation is more elongated. Within this structure, the body's center of gravity is lowered enough to provide a firm root balancing the weight of the upper body between both legs. Additionally, the practitioner's mobility and agility are not compromised as a result of a stance that is neither too rigid nor slow in response to the practitioner's reactions.

Cho ma (坐馬), or seated stance, is a modified version of what is commonly called sei ping ma (四平馬; four level stance), found in other Southern Chinese martial systems. This is the widely known *horse stance* that is used by many Asian arts to develop leg strength and stance stability. In Pak Mei, the legs are held close to the body compared to the broader versions of sei ping ma.

This enables quick transitions to take place as the Pak Mei practitioner shifts from one technique to another.

Diu ma (吊馬), translated as hanging stance, emphasizes a rear-legged base and light-footed lead leg posture. Commonly called the cat stance in English, the rear leg supports the actions of the lead leg within an evasive or attacking mode. Within Daai Jan Gwan, diu ma is typically employed in a transitional manner whereby the stance is not a set posture, but rather, a means of fluid and adaptable support.

Gwai ma (跪馬), the kneeling stance, enables the practitioner to descend to a lower fighting level without compromising his/her stability. This position is generally used to avoid an attack or to reinforce the strength of a practitioner's technique from a low vantage point. At times, the technique making use of this stance is very direct; in other instances, the stance is used to support stealthier staff strikes.

While the stances in the previously described paragraphs depict the postures found within the pole techniques of Daai Jan Gwan, the footwork refers to the movements in between the postures. Bou faat (步法), or stepping methods, can be viewed as anything and everything that takes place in between the stances. There are five primary methods of footwork employed in Daai Jan Gwan: wui (回; to return), teui (退; to retreat), cheung (搶; to charge), laai (拉; to pull), and tiu (跳; to leap). Properly executed footwork will enable a practitioner to simultaneously evade and attack by closing off the practitioner's vulnerable areas while creating opportunities in an opponent's defense.

In practice, each stance and footwork method is ascribed to a specific staff technique. In praxis, or actual application, stances and footwork are interchangeable with the staff techniques, creating a wider range of defensive and attacking maneuvers.

Sung: Dynamic Relaxation

The concept of sung (鬆), or to loosen, is perhaps the most important aspect in optimizing ging (勁), or integrated issuing force, in Pak Mei Kung Fu.

Within the domain of Chinese martial arts, Pak Mei is classified under the category of noi ga (內家), or internal family, Kung Fu. Typically, Taiji Quan (太極拳; Taai Gik Kyun in Cantonese), Bagua Zhang (八卦掌; Baat Gwa Jeung in Cantonese), and Xing Yi (形意; Ying Yi in Cantonese) form what is known as the internal arts triumvirate – the Big Three of Internal Chinese martial arts. In truth, there is nothing mysterious or mystical about the term *internal* as it is used to refer to Chinese martial arts. Internal can be summarized as understanding, implementing, and issuing the intrinsic energy that has been intentionally refined by an individual. Cultivating the concept of *qi* and its relationship with yi (意), leads to a maximized manifestation of ging. Initially, qi – defined as breath or vital energy in its most fundamental translation, must be consciously led by yi – the actively intelligent mind, to support the areas where ging will be expressed. As the qi begins to flow instinctively, efficiently, and effectively over time, it will energize the muscles and surrounding tissue so that the individual's body will be wholly strengthened. When sheer muscular strength is no longer necessary, qi no longer needs to be intentionally led by yi, and maximum force or power is issued from an integrated body, ging is achieved.

Returning to the principle of sung, relaxation is the key to maximizing qi flow. Sung should not be misconstrued as a limp or lifeless state. On the contrary, sung refers the loosening of the tissues and pathways through which qi flows so that tension will not obstruct the internal process. This is analogous to the water pressure in a garden hose. The water will flow at full strength when the hose is expanded and unfurled. Conversely, the water pressure can be stalled at a curl or kink in the hose, blocking the effectiveness of the full force of the flow.

Relaxation also endows the body with a vibrant and elastic quality whereby the issuance of force seems effortless. This is akin to the bounce in a basketball. A ball with a lively bounce has been filled efficiently. It requires very little effort from a player to display its rebounding property. On the other hand, an insufficiently-filled ball is considered dead – not enough air; little to no bounce. A ball of this condition demands a great amount of exertion from an individual to deliver a satisfactory level of bounce.

A body filled with an abundant supply of qi is said to have an effortless expression of ging, and sung is the means by which this can be achieved.

Luk Ging: The 6 Sectors of Kinetic Bridging

Luk Ging (六勁), or literally the six forces, refers to the 6 critical areas of the body that are identified as the key zones that activate the proper production and execution of ging in Pak Mei Kung Fu. Without compromising the underlying principle of whole body coordination and integrated force emission, these six areas have been defined differently within the diverse Pak Mei lineages. For example, Cheung Bing Lam (張炳林) – Cheung Lai Chuen's second son, classifies luk ging as: geuk (腳; legs), yiu (腰; waist), fuk (腹; abdomen), bok (膊; shoulders), sau (手; hands), and geng (頸; neck), while Cheung Bing Faat (張炳發) – Cheung's third son, determined that the six areas should be: geuk (腳; legs), yiu (腰; waist), bok (膊; shoulders), sau (手; hands), geng (頸; neck), and nga (牙; teeth).

Within the Kwong Man Fong lineage of Pak Mei Kung Fu, as with many others, the six sectors accountable for the physical aspect of generating force are: ma (馬; stance), yiu (腰; waist), bui (背; back), sau (手; hands), geng (頸; neck), and nga (牙; teeth). Their synchronous collaboration facilitates the optimum force that can be generated and issued within a Pak Mei technique. Each sector contributes to the continuum of force production by bridging or linking the significant portions of the body from the ground upward to complete the kinetic circuit. When an area successfully connects with the subsequent sector, the bridge by which the force travels is properly formed. For instance, when the stance is firmly rooted, the waist is able to receive and direct the force drawn from the stance. Conversely, should an area fail to sync properly with its counterparts, the force will be greatly compromised as a result of the improper bridging of the body's key components. For example, if a punch is thrown before the stance has been properly rooted, the force behind that punch will be minimal or even nonexistent. In this case, the power of the punch came principally from the arm's muscular action – known as lik (力), rather than the coordinated efforts of the entire body – known as ging.

At the highest levels of practice, all Pak Mei techniques are issued with ging rather than lik. This is particularly true of the way in which weapons are wielded – the integrated force needs to be issued from the coordinated efforts of the body's six sectors into the weapon for it to be efficiently and effectively executed. Otherwise, the success of the technique will be dependent solely upon sheer strength rather than a refined force that is indicative of luk ging.

Saam Ying: The Three Body Postures

There are three specific body postures, or ying (形), that provide ideal positioning in executing Pak Mei techniques: bin (扁; flat), bok (薄; thin), and yun (圓; round). In combat, these postures supply the structural support that will be able to accommodate the ging of a particular technique. While these postures are also found in the close-range hand methods of Pak Mei, they are employed differently within the context of a weapon – particularly the staff.

Bin, or flat, describes the practitioner's angled upright torso supporting the manipulation and propulsion of the staff. This positioning enables a practitioner to extend the staff's striking range while minimizing the practitioner's exposure to full frontal assaults from either armed or unarmed opponents. The pole's forward thrusting movements are reinforced by the weight and force of one side of the body directing the route of the strike. As a result, the leverage afforded by this posture supports techniques that lead with one particular side. With regard to defensive positioning, the practitioner's torso is turned to a side, effectively shielding the vital targets along at least one flank of the torso. This slim – or flat, posture enables a practitioner to guard one side of the body while simultaneously pursuing a counteroffensive with the other.

Bok, translated as thin, depicts a body posture that is perpendicular to an opponent's position. This thin shape confronts the opposition on a profile, or side-stance, strengthening the force of techniques from the sides of the body. Cho ma and teui bou, the seated stance and retreating footwork, respectively, are typically partnered with this upper body posture to support charging and retracting staff techniques. As a practitioner shifts into this posture, the pole can be used optimally to expose the opponent's vital areas or to suppress and subdue the opponent's attack. Defensively, bok ying – the thin posture, provides the practitioner with the most protection by revealing only the flank of the practitioner's body. The minimal exposure of vital points prevents an opponent from easily penetrating them.

Yun, or rounding, refers to the curvatures and arcs formed by the shoulders, back, and chest when this posture is used. The sinking and rising motions from the body's core region direct the force and course in which the staff will travel; and, the contraction of the chest cavity strengthens the force of staff strikes and reinforces expansive swings when a practitioner adopts the yun posture. The uniqueness of yun ying – the round shape, is that it is not only a posture, but a transitional form found in between pole maneuvers. Its function as both structure and segue makes yun an essential ying in wielding the staff in Pak Mei. On the defensive front, the curves and arcs of the upper body provide an effective structural brace to disperse the energy of direct attacks. While this may at times be interpreted as absorbing an attack, this structure ideally favors repulsing the energy of the incoming force or attack in the same manner that it is employed within hand techniques.

New York Pak Mei Kung Fu
Cultural Preservation Association

CHAPTER THREE

Daai Jan Gwan:

Principles of the Pole

"You must learn to be still in the midst of activity
and to be vibrantly alive in repose."
– Indira Gandhi,
Prime Minister of India
(1917-1984)

Staff Specifications

In general, the Pak Mei staff should have a personalized length approximately one forearm and hand length past the practitioner's height. While the quality of the wood can vary from a pliable wax wood to solid rosewood, each type plays a particular role in the stages of a practitioner's training.

Initially, a practitioner should train with a white wax pole. Called baak laap in Cantonese (白蠟; baila in Pinyin), the white wax wood is supple and springy – enabling the practitioner to transfer his/her integrated force throughout the weapon from the grip to its tip. In the beginning, it is important for the practitioner to *feel* the force travel through the pole in order to gain an understanding of the dimensions and distribution of energy in the staff. As the practitioner progresses toward an intermediate stage, a thicker rattan can be substituted to scaffold the individual's learning. With certain varieties of rattan, challenges in both density and dexterity will raise the individual's standard of practice. When the practitioner has gained proficiency in placing martial power along points on the pole and maneuvering the staff in an efficient manner, a hardwood pole can then be trained.

Mastery of the pole is characterized by the ease of control and the effortless issuance of force using any type of staff, flexible or firm. Although it is ultimately the practitioner's preference for a particular type of wooden staff, practice with all varieties of poles is highly recommended. Each kind of pole offers a different form and feeling due to its composition, and will broaden the practitioner's familiarity and versatility with the weapon.

Saam Gwaan

Saam gwaan (三關), or the three gates, refers to the concept that the staff is divided into three equally important sections. Tau gwaan (頭關), the lead gate, is the first third of the staff starting from the tip. The middle third of the staff is called yi gwaan (二關), or the second gate. The final segment of the staff closest to the practitioner's body is called saam gwaan (三關) – the third gate. An individual's integrated force travels through each stage of the staff during the application of a technique.

Tau gwaan is the top section of the pole primarily responsible for attacking maneuvers and checking movements. Concentrated staff strikes are channeled into the point, or dim (點), which is designated to target weak points and to attack vital areas found on the opponent. The tip of the staff – measured in the natural length of an individual's outstretched palm from the wrist to the fingertips, broadens the focus of force in which techniques can be employed. Attacks aimed at the limbs, hands, and head are effectively executed with this significant section of the staff. Dislocating the joints of an arm or leg, disarming an opponent's grip on a weapon, or jolting an opponent's crown with the side of the tip are typical maneuvers that are carried out by this portion of the staff.

Defensively, this anterior third of the pole can be used to redirect an incoming attack, consequently, regaining the advantage over an opponent during critical exchanges. Once contact is made, the practitioner combines intricate footwork with stifling staff methods to pressure the opponent into a vulnerable position. An experienced practitioner confidently awaits the opportunity to lure and lead an opponent into submission; an anxious apprentice searches for the openings and exploits the opponent's flaws. The understanding and mastery of tau gwaan is one key factor in determining the difference between the expert and the apprentice.

Yi gwaan is the middle segment of the staff that is the fulcrum of double-ended pole techniques. The hands are characteristically held at the boundaries of this third of the staff and balance both ends in maneuvers that are simultaneously defensive and offensive. When the practitioner's grip is positioned within yi gwaan, double-ended strikes can be executed in an unpredictable and stealthy manner. The body assumes a method of issuing integrated force throughout the pole that is different from single-ended strikes.

Since the pole, itself, and the pair of ends are close to the practitioner's body, an understanding of manipulating the pole using the body's natural weight in tandem with the principles of torsion will maximize the effectiveness of seung tau staff techniques. Strategic placement of the body's weight behind movements – also known as weight-bearing, bolsters the force of staff strikes with the ends of the pole. The lead leg and leading shoulder should direct and support the striking end of the pole. Backed by the physical weight of this side of the body, the strength of this frontal striking end is fortified.

At the same time, torsion – or the spiraling force inherent in all Pak Mei techniques, facilitates ging, amplifying the efficiency of double-ended pole techniques. The turning, torques, and twisting motions increase the striking potential of seung tau methods. Once the stance is secure, the turning of the waist initiates the sequence of force production in the upper body. The energy then spirals through the arms, transferring to the twisting movements of the staff. With an extended range of approximately two feet beyond the flanks of the body, staff strikes with either end of the pole will typically perform clubbing and thrashing motions while staff strokes will characteristically execute stripping and severing maneuvers.

Saam gwaan is the section that links the practitioner with the pole during single-ended staff techniques. The left hand is characteristically held at the edge of the base of the staff while the right hand is positioned at the border of this third of the weapon. The grip on the staff needs to be firm yet flexible so that the practitioner is able to wield the weapon with both control and ging. Relaxation in between the crisp movements enables the staff to move in a lively and powerful manner. Conversely, tightly held grips transfer the might of muscular strength rather than the effectiveness of integrated force. This is a skill that is trained through drills and gained from experience.

From this grip position, the staff can be handled like a seesaw, propped upward like the font end of a forklift, or waved in the manner of a flag. When the staff held within this section is wielded in one direction, the radial range is approximately four feet. This means that when a practitioner executes a dan tau technique, the distance that the technique can cover is approximately four feet away from the body with a standard seventy-two inch staff – the distance will understandably be longer if the staff is longer. This extended reach requires the practitioner to master the mechanics that can effectively project ging into and throughout the pole while instantaneously executing the technique at the opposite end of the weapon. Upward tilts, downward strikes, and lifting attacks are commonly used from the single-ended position, empowering the tip of the yi gwaan with the lethal applications. When the practitioner executes a sweep, or swing around the entire body, the diametric range is extended to approximately nine feet. This enables the practitioner to ward off attackers up to a distance of nine feet from one end of the swing to the other as it revolves around the practitioner's body. Essentially, the practitioner is able to simultaneously defend and attack an upwards of four and one-half feet in any and every direction during the course of a sweeping technique.

Yin and Yang

The notion of yin and yang (陰陽; pronounced yam yeung in Cantonese) is possibly the most influential concept underlying the Chinese mindset. It is a philosophical construct that can be used either to express in simplest terms the duality of nature or even to explain the complex dynamics of the creation of the universe. On the most elemental level, yin is viewed as an inactive state associated with passiveness, darkness, winter, night, and the female while yang is considered active in affiliation with activity, light, summer, daytime, and the male, respectively.

Neither yin nor yang is ever completely devoid of the other – much like the relationship between night and day. The interaction of these opposites leads to an alternating cycle of decline or ascendancy by either of these forces in a dynamic balancing act adhering to natural laws. While an element or condition within the yin-yang dynamic may innately be yin or yang, its relationship to its counterpart determines its position as yin or yang within the interplay. In other words, the context decides whether the matter in question will be yin or yang, not whether something is fundamentally yin or yang. For example, a defensive maneuver such as a block which is typically considered *yin* can be actively *yang* as it responds in an offensive manner to an attack. In terms of cause and consequence, when a situation reaches an extreme, it will convert to its opposite. This effectively offsets the potential dominance of one condition over its complement. For instance, day turns to night, and night to day. Within Pak Mei, the principle of yin and yang is one of the tenets that define this martial art.

The notions of complementary positioning, balancing forces, and corresponding actions are manifested from this pervasive concept in Chinese martial arts. The hand placement on the staff is said to assume a yin and yang arrangement: at rest in upright position, the fingers of the left grip at the base of the staff face the right side of the body while the fingers of the right grip further up the staff face the left side of the body. The hands oppose each other in placement, but assist each other in movement. With regard to strategic proximity, an individual is considered to be in the yin phase of combat when he/she is vulnerable to attacks. Conversely, the yang phase enables a practitioner to take advantage of the opportunity to strike. It is important to note that these are merely phases and that a simple sidestep or skillful counter-maneuver can quickly change the dynamic of the situation to its other extreme: from yin to yang, to yang to yin.

In terms of physical dimensions, yin and yang can be used to address active and passive areas throughout the body and the staff that contribute to a systemic balance. While techniques are executed, the practitioner's body parts constantly experience an interchange between yin and yang. When a practitioner repositions a foot to the rear to avoid a low attack, this is considered yin. As he/she simultaneously attacks with the staff, this portion of the body is in a state of yang. Although the two sections of the body are engaged in two different motions – defensive and offensive, respectively, the yin and yang dynamic instills a global balance within the individual's framework as the technique is employed. Accordingly, during double-ended pole techniques, the deflective blocking end is in the yin phase while the simultaneous striking end assumes a yang status. The angular diffusion and finesse used to diffuse an incoming attack is considered passive and yielding which is characteristic of yin; on the other hand, the forceful and vigorous strike supported by the active and weight-bearing side of the body signifies the nature of yang. Again, these alternations between yin and yang are amorphous as they constantly shift and change within the different contexts and settings.

As it relates to the composition of a technique, yin is found in the aftermath of a technique while yang would be considered the actual execution of it. The waning period of an offensive maneuver is considered an inactive state which maintains a yin association. In contrast, the strike, itself, is the active condition that represents a yang state. Ideally, one would attack the opponent's yin condition – the weakened phase of a strike, and the recovery and regrouping period leading into the subsequent technique. Knowing this, the practitioner must also be aware of his/her own yin states in order to appropriately defend against attacks targeted at these junctures. A skilled exponent has either studied and cultivated this understanding or naturally has an innate ability to apply these principles.

Baat Ging, Baat Faat

Baat ging (八勁) – the eight forces, and baat faat (八法) – the eight methods, refers to the eight principle manners in which the staff is used and the eight primary applications for those eight movements in Daai Jan Gwan. When luk ging is proficiently performed, the ability to produce force is established. The issuing force can assume 8 mannerisms – meaning how this force will be used within the framework of a staff technique. Each characteristic conveys a unique way in which the force can be utilized. While baat ging occurs during the execution of a Pak Mei technique, its application is defined by baat faat. These principles are better known as The Eight Actions and Eight Applications.

Baat ging highlights eight specific staff actions: tiu (挑), saat (殺), seut (摔), jong (撞), paau (抛), paak (拍), sou (掃), and hyun (圈). For each action, there is a literal translation and a martial interpretation. Both versions will be presented for clarity and precision.

Tiu literally means to carry on a pole. Its martial application is a lifting action that is compared to the rising motion of a seesaw.

Saat means to kill. While it is intended to be a finishing strike, saat takes the form of a downward striking maneuver.

Seut is literally interpreted as to fall onto the ground. The martial action is a forward thrust.

Jong means to knock against or to bump into. Martially, it means to ram with the base end of the staff.

Paau is literally translated as to throw or toss. The martial implication is to drive upward, essentially throwing the body upward while leading the staff in that direction.

Paak means to beat or hit. It is a striking action that uses the frontal third of the staff to perform its namesake.

Sou means to sweep or clear away. A large sweep with the staff is intended to clear away the area and eliminate any obstructions.

Hyun is to encircle or loop around. The use of the staff in a circular pattern dissipates the energy of an attack or builds momentum in a forward attack.

Baat faat explains the eight primary applications of the eight actions: chyun (穿), seui (碎), saak (塞), lau (漏), lak (勒), pek(劈), fan (分), and mo (摩). Again, for each action, there is a literal translation and a martial interpretation. Both versions will once again be represented.

Chyun means to pierce. In the martial sense, chyun means to penetrate with the staff, not just to strike.

Seui is to smash or break into pieces. Any strike should have the capability to smash or break something into pieces upon impact.

Saak is literally translated as to stop or to seal. The staff needs to be wielded in a manner that will not only block an attack, but will seal off any subsequent reprisals.

Lau means to leak or drip. It suggests stealth and proposes to get under an attack and to emerge with not only the advantage, but the finishing maneuver.

Lak is to strangle. With a staff, the function is not to strangle, but to ensnare or to tie up in an arresting manner.

Pek is to split or chop. Any striking action with the staff should have the ability to split or sever the area attacked.

Fan is to divide. The application is to partition the opponent's body parts: stance, waist, and arms from each other, in order to prevent a unified ability to attack.

Mo literally means to grind. In the martial sense, mo means to strip or tear away. A weapon or any extremity will be stripped away when the staff is wielded in this way.

The wide-ranging implications of baat ging baat faat are that a myriad of permutations can arise from the combinations of these actions and applications. In other words, an action can be combined with any application amplifying the quantity and quality of staff maneuvers.

For instance, paau – an upward motion, can have a smashing application – seui, a separating application – fan, or any other of the remaining six faat. Understandably, some applications may not ideally correspond with one of the eight actions. However, the possibilities and interpretations are left to the initiative and cleverness of those able to recognize the magnitude of options available in Daai Jan Gwan.

CHAPTER FOUR

Daai Jan Gwan:

The Form

"拳怕少壯, 棍怕老郎"

Kyun pa siu jong, gwan pa lou long

(With the fist, fear the young and robust;

with the pole, fear the experienced master)

– Kung Fu proverb

The sequence of Daai Jan Gwan represented in this chapter stems from the Hong Kong lineage of Pak Mei Kung Fu. While practitioners may have revisions, alterations, or deletions pertaining to this form due to personal preferences or individualized instruction, the principles remain the same.

Each photograph depicts the best viewing position of each posture, but not necessarily the correct direction in which the technique is actually executed within the form.

The proper direction will be represented by one of eight gwa (卦) – traditionally, the divinatory trigrams derived from the four phenomena originating from yin and yang: greater yang, lesser yin; lesser yang, greater yin.

乾	kin	Northwest
坤	kwan	Southwest
辰	san	East
坎	ham	North
艮	gan	Northeast
巽	seun	Southeast
離	lei	South
兌	deui	West

Daai Jan Gwan
大陣棍

1. 開樁: Hoi jong
   朝天一柱香   Chiu tin yat chyu heung
2. 退馬殺棍   Teui ma saat gwan
3. 逼步摔棍   Bik bou seut gwan
4. 回馬殺棍   Wui ma saat gwan
5. 斜馬挑棍   Che ma tiu gwan
6. 拉馬殺棍   Laai ma saat gwan
7. 逼步箭棍   Bik bou jin gwan
8. 卍字馬拍棍   Maan ji ma paak gwan
9. 轉身標棍   Jyun san biu gwan
10. 回馬撞棍   Wui ma jong gwan
11. 瀉馬腰封   Se ma yiu fung gwan
12. 退馬拍棍   Teui ma paak gwan
13. 卍字馬達棍   Maan ji ma daat gwan
14. 瀉馬盪棍   Se ma dong gwan
15. 瀉馬橫掃棍   Se ma waang sou gwan
16. 逼步撞棍   Bik bou jong gwan
17. 瀉馬腰封   Se ma yiu fung gwan
18. 吊馬啄棍   Diu ma deuk gwan
19. 跪馬虎尾棍   Gwai ma fu mei gwan

20. 轉身掃棍	Jyun san sou gwan
21. 落跪壓棍	Lok gwai ngaat gwan
22. 瀉馬拋棍	Se ma paau gwan
23. 拉馬殺棍	Laai ma saat gwan
24. 搶步標棍	Cheung bou biu gwan
25. 轉身殺棍	Jyun san saat gwan
26. – 46.	(repeat #3 – 23)
47. 吊馬漏水棍	Diu ma lau seui gwan
48. 飛身圈棍	Fei san waan gwan
49. 落馬摔棍	Lok ma seut gwan
50. 跳步圓棍	Tiu bou hyun gwan
51. 車身拍棍	Che san paak gwan
52. 上馬撞棍	Seung ma jong gwan
53. 轉身殺棍	Jyun san saat gwan
54. 搶步箭棍	Cheung bou jin gwan
55. 回身轉棍	Wui san jyun gwan
56. 收樁	Sau jong

40

1. Hoi jong: Chiu tin yat chyu heung

   開樁: 朝天一柱香

   Opening position: Face the sky with one pillar of incense

   Face east with the base of the staff resting on the right leg just above the knee in the Pak Mei stance.

(Frontal view)

2. Teui ma saat gwan

退馬殺棍

Move back into a stance; killing staff

Shift the left foot toward the rear so that the right foot is positioned as the lead foot facing north. The staff strikes downward.

3. Bik bou seut gwan

逼步摔棍

Pressing step; thrusting staff

Step forward and drive the staff ahead in a Pak Mei stance.

4. Wui ma saat gwan

回馬殺棍

Returning stance; killing staff

Shift into the previous side-stance and strike the staff downward.

5. Che ma tiu gwan

斜馬挑棍

Slanted stance; carrying staff

Pivot into a Pak Mei stance facing northeast. Strike upward with the staff.

6. Laai ma saat gwan

拉馬殺棍

Pulling stance; killing staff

Pivot on the right foot to the northwest. Strike downward with the staff.

7. Bik bou jin gwan

逼步箭棍

Pressing step; lunging staff

Step forward shifting into a Pak Mei stance. Thrust the staff forward in the direction of the step.

8. Maan ji ma paak gwan

卍字馬拍棍

Stance in the shape of the dharmic swastika character; striking staff

The right leg and foot shifts behind the left leg into a modified cross-legged stance.

The staff rotates downward toward the left, blocking and striking simultaneously.

9. Jyun san biu gwan

轉身標棍

Turning body; projecting staff

Turn counter-clockwise to the right, stepping into a stance facing south. The staff projects outward from the side of the body.

10. Wui ma jong gwan

回馬撞棍

Returning stance; ramming staff

Step to the left, facing north. Slide the staff through the left grip, thrusting the base of the staff outward from the side of the body at shoulder level.

11. Se ma yiu fung gwan

瀉馬腰封

Swiftly shifting stance; waist sealing staff

The left foot shifts outward to the side into a Pak Mei stance facing north. The secured stance enables the waist to initiate the force in the upper body. The staff swings to the upper left side.

12. Teui ma paak gwan

退馬拍棍

Move back into a stance; striking staff

The left foot steps back into a Pak Mei stance. The staff shifts into a double-ended position, striking downward with the left end of the pole.

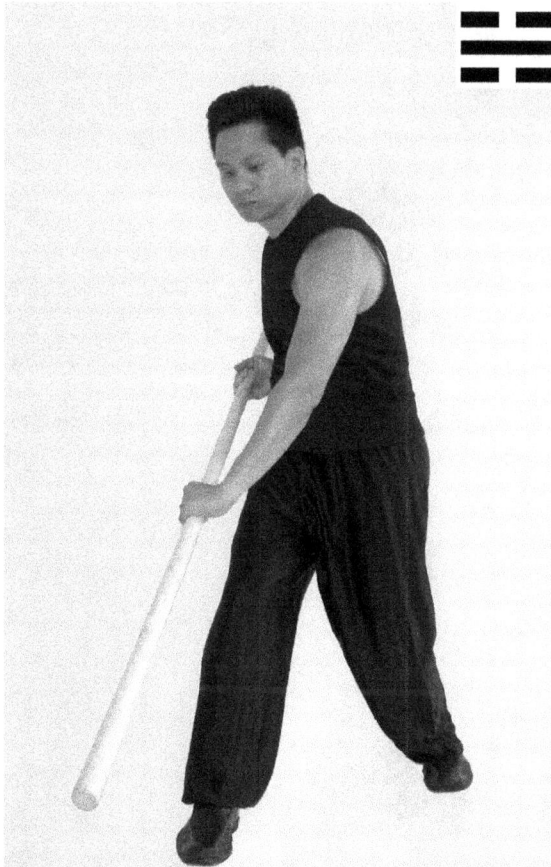

13. Maan ji ma daat gwan

卍字馬達棍

Stance in the shape of the dharmic swastika character; conquering staff

The right leg crosses the left leg into a modified cross-legged stance. The staff returns to a single-ended position, striking downward toward the left, which is the northwest compass direction – in this case, the kin gwa.

14. Se ma dong gwan

瀉馬盪棍

Swiftly shifting stance; swinging staff

The right foot steps to the right. The staff swings to the upper right side.

15. Se ma waang sou gwan

瀉馬橫掃棍

Swiftly shifting stance; sweeping away staff

The left foot steps forward into a seated stance, supporting a counter-clockwise sweeping movement ending with the base of the staff facing west.

16. Bik bou jong gwan

逼步撞棍

Pressing step; ramming staff

The left foot steps toward the left, or west. Slide the staff through the left grip, thrusting the base of the staff outward from the side of the body at shoulder level.

17. Se ma yiu fung gwan

瀉馬腰封

Swiftly shifting stance; waist sealing staff

The left foot steps forward into a Pak Mei stance facing north. The secured stance enables the waist to initiate the force in the upper body. The staff swings to the upper left side.

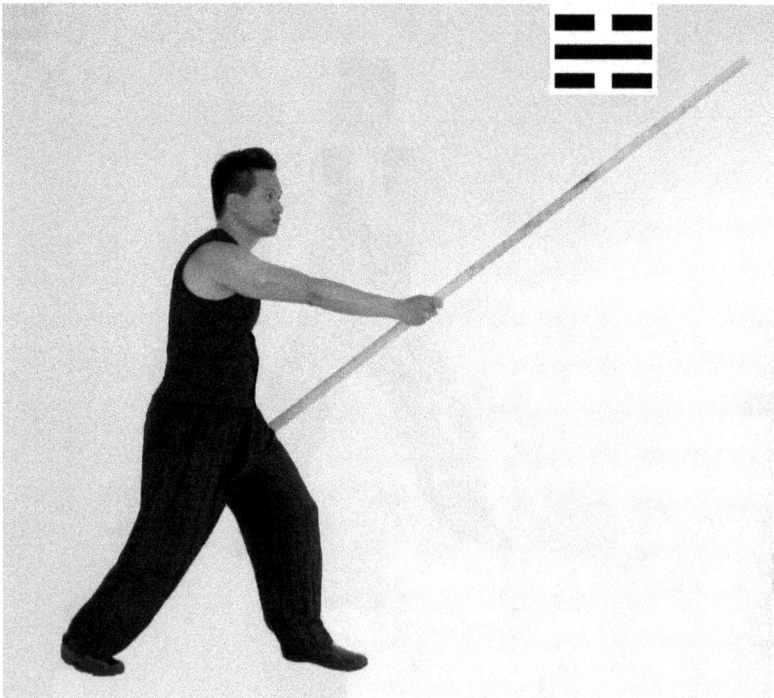

18. Diu ma deuk gwan

吊馬啄棍

Hanging stance; pecking staff

The right foot steps forward into a hanging stance with the left leg bearing the bulk of the weight of the stance. The staff pivots on the right grip, rotating downward with the tip striking the ground.

19. Gwai ma fu mei gwan

跪馬虎尾棍

Kneeling stance; tiger tail staff

The right leg shifts back into a kneeling stance to support an upward strike toward the rear. This technique is executed in the southern direction.

20. Jyun san sou gwan

轉身掃棍

Turning body; sweeping staff

Facing north, stand up into a Pak Mei stance with the left foot forward. Sweep the staff overhead in one complete counter-clockwise motion.

21. Lok gwai ngaat gwan

落跪壓棍

Dropping stance; pressing staff

Drop into a kneeling stance facing north with the staff lain in front of the body.

22. Se ma paau gwan

瀉馬拋棍

Swiftly shifting stance; casting staff

The right foot shifts back into a Pak Mei stance, facing forward, in this case, still northward. The staff is propped upward with the full support of the body behind it.

23. Laai ma saat gwan

拉馬殺棍

Pulling stance; killing staff

The left foot steps back, supporting a downward strike in the northern direction.

24. Cheung bou biu gwan

搶步標棍

Charging step; projecting staff

Charge forward with the right foot into a stance supporting a staff thrust outward to the side – again, facing north.

25. Jyun san saat gwan

轉身殺棍

Turning body; killing staff

The body pivots on the left foot, turning and striking downward with the staff after the right foot steps to the left. The direction of the technique has now changed from north to south.

26– 46.   Repeat the sequence from techniques numbered 3. – 23.

47. Diu ma deuk gwan

吊馬漏水棍

Hanging stance; pecking staff

The right foot steps forward into a hanging stance with the left leg bearing the bulk of the weight of the stance. The staff pivots on the right grip, rotating downward with the tip striking the ground.

48. Fei san waan gwan

飛身圈棍

Quickly darting body; encircling staff

Step forward with the left foot and vault off this same foot, enabling the right foot to charge forward. At the same time, the staff is held in front of the body, circling in a counter-clockwise manner.

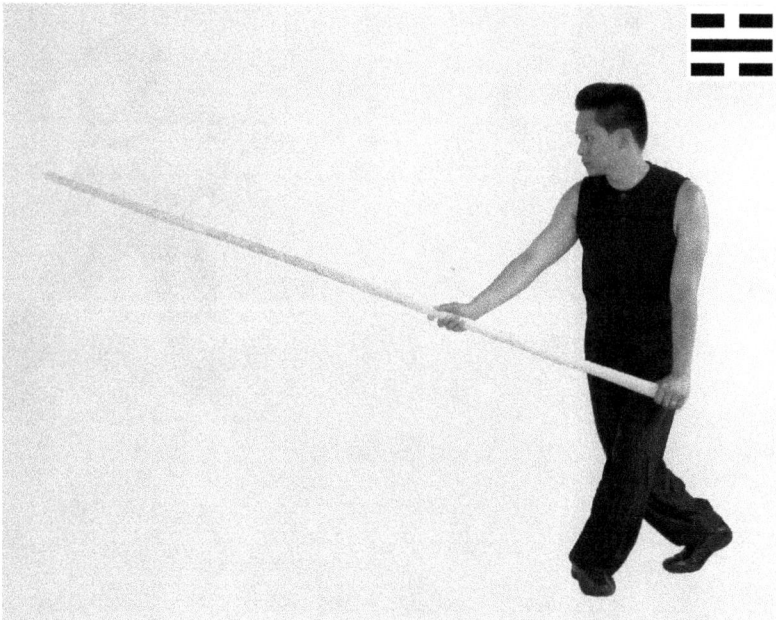

49. Lok ma seut gwan

落馬摔棍

Dropping stance; thrusting staff

The right foot steps down into a stance while the staff thrusts forward.

50. Tiu bou hyun gwan

跳步圍棍

Leaping step; circling staff

Step back with the right leg crossing the left leg. Vault off the right foot after stepping down; the left foot hops to the rear. At the same time, the staff is held in front of the body, circling in a clockwise manner.

51. Che san paak gwan

車身拍棍

Carting body; striking staff

The right foot steps to the rear, causing the body to face east. The staff is retracted to a double-ended position with the technique facing northeast.

52. Seung ma jong gwan

上馬撞棍

Forward stance; ramming staff

Charge forward: step to the left with the left foot – which is facing north. With the support of the stance, the base end of the pole is propelled from the side in an upward direction.

53. Jyun san saat gwan

轉身殺棍

Turning body; killing staff

Step forward with the right foot into a stance supporting a downward strike. The body is now facing west; however, the staff technique is directed north.

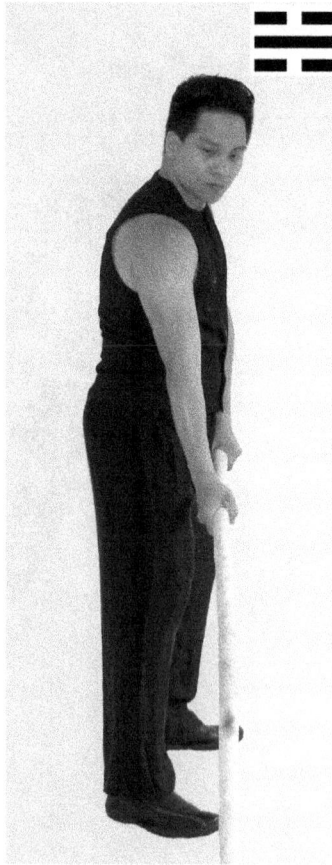

54. Cheung bou jin gwan

搶步箭棍

Charging step; lunging staff

Charge forward with the right foot, again in the northern direction. The stepping supports a thrusting staff in front of the body.

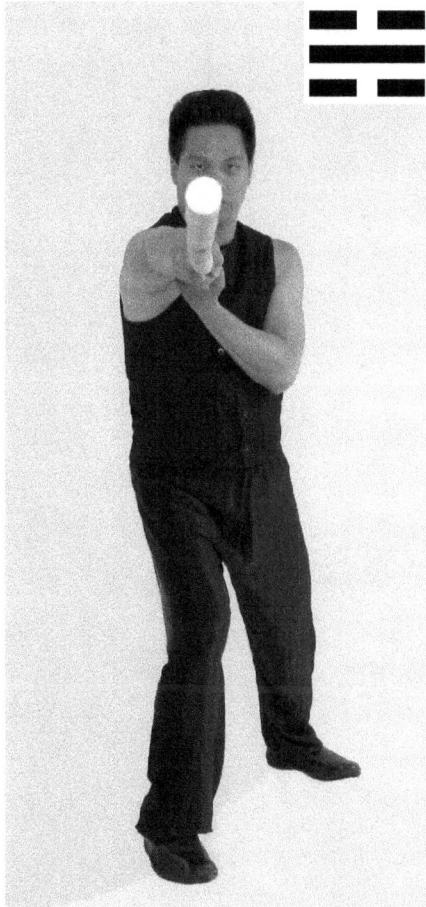

55. Wui san jyun gwan

回身轉棍

Returning body; turning staff

Step back with the right leg which bears the bulk of the weight of the stance. Withdraw the staff, rotating the staff in a clockwise direction.

56. Sau jong

收樁

Closing position

The left palm extends forward in a closing salute. The staff is cradled in the right arm.

CHAPTER FIVE

Individualized Understandings

&

Combative Concepts

"It is you and your skill, not your system,

that will be the source of your success in a physical conflict."

– Marc "Animal" MacYoung,

Founder of

No Nonsense Self-Defense

Daai Jan Gwan is a form – a sequence of techniques that have been strung together in an ideal manner to familiarize a practitioner of Pak Mei Kung Fu with an efficient and effective set of staff methods. It needs to be *studied* in order to be used productively; otherwise, it is reduced to a mere series of martially aesthetic movements – as the case may be with any kyun, or form.

Attentiveness to one's personal attributes and alertness to oppositional weaknesses are essential in manifesting the concepts and principles associated with effective techniques. To place this within a practical perspective, techniques favoring the right side, in all likelihood, will not be as efficient for a left-handed practitioner. Combined with a teacher who emphasizes only one way of executing the technique, the exponent will have further obstacles to overcome, and undo, in the process of realizing that he/she must customize the method in order for it to function in a maximized manner. The application of a technique for a five-foot tall slender female would be very different from the application of the same technique for a six-foot-four-inch tall muscular male. For others with inherent abilities or impairments of sorts, understanding and adapting is an essential function of daily living. In many respects, they are able to customize more comfortably and quickly than those who follow instruction in a very direct and rigid manner.

The key to unlocking the potential of formalized instruction is to learn the method, think critically, and to interpret the technique for individualized implementation. The function of a technique can and will vary from individual to individual. There is no one-size-fits-all technique, but there are different ways in which a technique can and should be applied. This understanding in itself is a talent for some and a learning experience for others. This chapter will explore the ways to facilitate the awareness that is vital to an individual's martial growth and personal development.

Jaam Gwan

Jaam jong (站樁), also known as standing post, is practiced by many Chinese martial arts to establish the skill of properly aligning and understanding the body, storing the qi, and revitalizing the practitioner's essence. Jaam gwan (站棍), or standing staff, teaches the practitioner to interact with the staff in a similar manner. Each posture in Daai Jan Gwan is able to be held in a static position to attain the same energizing and enlightening properties of jaam jong. In jaam gwan, there are three progressive stages that address corrective alignment, energetic development, and transitional efficacy.

In the initial stage, the practitioner learns to understand the properties of the body with the staff at rest. Standing with the staff enables the practitioner to identify the center of gravity for each final position, and allows natural influences such as gravity and physiology to bring the body to a state of equilibrium. Quite often, these two factors are compromised either by unobserved efforts to compensate for strength or intentional endeavors to avoid pain. As a result, the mind directs the body to perform movements in manners that are advantageous in the short-term, but become rather counterproductive in the long run. In time, these compensative behaviors form bad habits that can lead to other impairments. By aligning the stance with the staff in a manner that makes the most of gravitational forces and enhanced body positioning, the practitioner is able to regain a sense of physiological normalcy and establish the physical prerequisites that will ideally optimize the performance of staff techniques.

Realignment follows the same principles that are found in Pak Mei empty-handed postures: the center of gravity must be lowered; the shoulders must be dropped; and the elbows must be sunken. These are all physiological features that act harmoniously with the nature of gravity. Furthermore, each physical characteristic maintains a practical purpose. A low center of gravity will lighten the load along with other stressors that can affect the upper body while securing the stance so that an integrated force can be initiated from this sector of the body. This enables the upper body to maintain a supple and relaxed state, capable of executing techniques in a maximized manner. Defensively, the low center of gravity also prevents the practitioner from being uprooted by the opposition. Elevated shoulders create tension in the trapezius muscles – the set of flat muscles on each side of the shoulders, back, and upper and back parts of the neck. Tension in this area can impede performance as well as lead to chronic injuries. Sunken elbows support integrated force by eliminating the tension that can be accumulated from elbows that flair out to the sides which increase a dependency on muscles rather than rely on correct alignment. This positioning also allows the staff to stay close to the body so that the practitioner can maintain a better sense of control of the pole.

As the practitioner progresses and the postures become stronger, the practitioner moves onto the stage of energy development to support staff techniques. The internal aspect of Pak Mei Kung Fu requires internal cultivation in order to sustain and reinforce the external manifestation of force within the system's techniques. The concept of *internal* addresses: an ability to develop qi and optimize its implementation on a metaphysical level; the capacity to generate force in an integrated manner which encompasses the entire body on a physical level; the faculty to unify the metaphysical with the physical to bolster the external expression of techniques on a psychological level; and, the promotion of personal enlightenment within a spiritual context. This phase of jaam gwan provides the practitioner with the opportunity to direct all attention to the relationship between the practitioner and the pole. This intimacy leads to the internal refinement that is required to wield the staff effectively.

The legs are strengthened through the stances in each posture, thereby, lowering the center of gravity and sinking the qi. The rooting of the stance secures the foundation so that the upper body is able to maintain a supple quality to maximize the transfer of force into the staff. Aside from the grip, there is minimal muscle use in the holding of each posture. This promotes the sinuous properties of the waist and extremities to lead movements in a more energy-efficient manner. At the same time, the cultivation of qi within the daan tin (丹田; dan tian in Pinyin) – the energy center, literally the cinnabar field, that is located approximately three finger-widths below the naval, is activated and attuned to the positions of the staff. Since the body becomes familiar with the postures from jaam gwan, the qi can be led to energize these pertinent positions with ease and proficiency. As the internal characteristics are strengthened, the external expression is enhanced, leading to improved performance and the vigorous execution of techniques.

In the advanced stage of jaam gwan, the idea of *movement in stillness* is realized. When a practitioner has been able to cultivate and circulate the qi, and the body has been sufficiently strengthened, the energy flowing through the body's circulatory channels evolves the individual – globally. As a result, awareness transforms to enlightenment and techniques transcend performance. This means that at this phase of mastery, the principles of effectiveness and efficiency are ingrained in the practitioner. The technique and the individual are indistinguishable, exemplifying the harmonious connection between the mind, body, and spirit. During jaam gwan at this level, the practitioner's thinking has developed into instinct, and the methods and means of techniques are actively explored in this meditative state. The circulation of the qi is considered the movement, and the posture held during jaam gwan is in stillness. Even though the body is at rest during jaam gwan, the energetic activity of the qi stimulates mental acuity and promotes precision in the execution of techniques.

With regard to the manifestation of staff methods, jaam gwan refines techniques and fashions a multitude of permutations for the applications. Performing pole techniques trains the movements; and, standing with the postures polishes the methods. Gross motor movements carried out by a novice are reduced to stealthy subtle motions achieved by an expert. As a result, this decreases telegraphic movements and facilitates faster transitions between techniques. The insightfulness that arises at this level of jaam gwan enables the practitioner to envision further offensive and defensive possibilities for standardized staff maneuvers. Typically, the mindset of the traditional sifu was to teach one primary application per technique which was emphasized as the sole purpose of the technique. This was characteristically the conventional manner in which a hok sang (學生) – or student, learned until he/she was accepted as a tou dai (徒弟) – or disciple. In the liberated state of jaam gwan, the individual is free to discover and unlock the limitless potential encrypted within techniques. It is important to note, however, that at this level of awareness, the techniques and their applications become personalized, meaning that what may work for one practitioner may not work for another in the same manner. While the various possibilities exist, adapting and emphasizing the effective execution of techniques remains a constant source of revision and refinement that is furnished by jaam gwan.

Standing staff is not meant to be a mere foundational activity that will be abandoned when the practitioner has reached a level of proficiency in its implementation. Jaam gwan is actually a process that reinforces each stage of a practitioner's progress. It defines the effort and perseverance that is vital to the pursuit of *Kung Fu*.

Ging: Training Integrated Force

The metaphysical preparation provided by jaam gwan is balanced by the practitioner's physical training with the pole. Once the body has been primed to support the demands of issuing force through the staff without causing personal injury, the practitioner is able to embark upon a study of efficient movements with the staff – the maximized motions in between the postures.

There are characteristically three phases to the performance of any technique: ignition, action, and completion. As a beginner, these stages are very exaggerated and visible – similar to a budding toddler working toward a mastery of walking. As progress is made, these phases become less apparent and assume a seamless state within the action. At the mastery level, the phases of motion within a technique are considered invisible and instantaneous – comparable to the frame by frame illustrations on the pages of a flip-it book, whereby each image on each page represents the completion of each motion. The highest achievement for a practitioner is when instinct and action become indivisible.

Ging expression in the staff begins with proper physiological alignment. Correct physical configurations support ging while unstable bodily features emphasize muscular manipulation and premature fatigue. At the onset of a technique, it is important to accentuate the acceleration of the staff. This initial vigor is required to appropriately energize the staff movement. Without such intensified liveliness to unleash the technique, the force will not be effectively expressed in the action phase of the movement. Consequently, the staff will not produce any martial power; the motion will be detected and countered by the opponent; and, the practitioner's efforts would have been wasted.

The action phase is characteristically the intended application of the technique. Once the force has been initiated and has been given a direction, the technique is realized in the action. The staff implements the design of the technique in the manner in which it was launched. A crisp action produces the desired application; a weak stroke yields a compromising position.

The completion of the motion is perhaps the least considered aspect of the technique. The follow-through phase of a motion is of particular importance during practice since it is during training that one can safely perform and explore the dynamics of a technique. Completing the technique involves going beyond the action phase to accentuate the penetration of the staff. To end a technique in the action phase and segue into the subsequent movement without the follow-through is to pull the technique. Pulling checks the strength of the force needed to properly execute the movement. Prolonged training without regard for this critical phase will lead to the ineffectual implementation of these techniques in actual use. The follow-through is the follow-up to a technique, ensuring direction, infiltration, and finality.

While the completion phase ends one technique, it leads to the birth of the next one. This cycle must be implemented throughout the entire form during practice in order for one to ensure integrated force issuance within every technique. Accordingly, actual applications are invigorated and amplified with the infusion of ging.

Sang Mun/ Sei Mun: Live Gate/Dead Gate

Personal practice develops fluency with the staff while combative concepts provide essential insights into strategic positioning and tactical execution.

The notion of sang mun/sei mun (生門/死門), or live gate/dead gate, refers to adverse and advantageous engagement, respectively, during combat. When the practitioner is in a position where the opponent can both attack effectively and guard successfully, this is considered the live gate. Sang mun is an unfavorable situation for the practitioner, yet an opportune condition for the opponent. The practitioner will find it difficult to capitalize on techniques that are executed in this gate since the opponent has the means to both evade and counterattack. Sei mun, on the other hand, exploits the opponent's powerlessness against the practitioner's strategically well-positioned attack. The dead gate represents the areas that the opponent would have difficulty defending during an attack. Inexperienced fighters typically reveal their sei mun unknowingly through the manner in which they carry themselves. An uncertain demeanor, the favoring of a particular side, or impatient and impulsive attacks are all telltale signs that a dead gate can be targeted for the practitioner to exploit. Conversely, seasoned practitioners understand the dangers associated with this gate and close it at every opportunity.

Exposing a dead gate is achieved through a combination of footwork mobility and the subtle movements of the staff. The use of angular patterns, better known as baat gwa bou (八卦步; 8 diagram steps), to enhance the primary methods of footwork employed

88

in Daai Jan Gwan: wui, teui, cheung, laai, and tiu, provides the means to infiltrate the dead gate. These evasive and aggressive stepping methods allow a practitioner to elude attacks and reengage assertively. Additionally, this dynamic stepping approach addresses two essential elements pertaining to distance: proximity and range. Within this context, proximity refers to the position of the practitioner relative to the opponent while range represents the striking distance. A live gate becomes a dead gate when the practitioner has effectively maneuvered into a position that will stifle an opponent's ability to react constructively with regard to proximity and which will create opportunities for the practitioner to attack decisively in relation to range.

Practitioners experienced with the pole naturally execute techniques with a sense of positioning, timing, and accuracy. These staff skills enable the practitioner to penetrate the sei mun once the proximity and range have been secured by the footwork. Effective staff placement, or positioning, enables the practitioner to control the course of the technique. The perfectly-placed staff bears weight on the opponent, secures the extremities, and strikes a vital target – simultaneously, which are outcomes developed from understanding and experience. Solid staff placement is further reinforced by timing. Uncalculated efforts can be telegraphed to the opponent who can, in turn, contain and counter the practitioner's technique – no matter how sophisticated the technique may be. Staff methods which are well-timed challenge an opponent's reactive responsiveness and create opportunities for mistakes to be made; and, when an opening in sei mun has been revealed, a precise attack completes the technique. Accuracy manifests the practitioner's intent, objective, and expertise while it validates the aim of the technique. The dead gate is a means to an opponent's defeat, and the knowledge and ability to exploit it can lead to the opponent's demise.

Saam Mun: The Three Doors

Saam mun (三門), or three doors, refers to the three lateral zones of the body that have been designated as both regions of attack and defense. These partitioned zones outline the geography of vital areas on the body. Furthermore, they are the foundation upon which the map of finer vital points rest.

The upper door is known as seung mun (上門). This zone consists of the head and upper chest region. Within this door, the vital targets located on the face and the meridians running along the upper chest are the primary areas to both attack and defend. Typically, eager opponents will immediately attack this door in pursuit of landing the famous knockout blow. As a result, seung mun is generally the most guarded as well as most sought after region during a physical altercation.

The middle door is identified as jung mun (中門). This central zone is comprised of the body's primary internal organs. Accordingly, many sensitive points and critical cavities can be targeted within this region to cause an opponent serious injury. Conversely, due to the vulnerability of this area, a highly effective defense needs to be in place to protect the ribs and viscera of this region. Of the three doors, this sector raises the most concern due to the abundance of vital points that can harm either the opponent or the practitioner.

Ha mun (下門) is the term used to refer to the lower door. This section is the source of the individual's foundation – the stance and footwork. While this region is primarily composed of the lower extremities, the legs, a primary vital area in this zone is the groin – in particular, the highly sensitive testes. The strategic positioning of an individual's legs throughout various stances can effectively shield the groin area from attacks. Furthermore, the mobility and maneuverability of the footwork enables the individual to evade risky situations or engage in opportune encounters. Attacks to the legs are typically designed to trip, trap or maim an individual. An experienced practitioner can open the other doors by entering through this one first.

The staff methods aimed at high, medium, and low levels concentrate on specific targets housed within these zones. The practice of infiltrating the dead gate and attacking the points and cavities within these doors outlines the overarching strategy of staff methods in Chinese martial arts.

CHAPTER SIX

Traditional Training Methods

"There are no shortcuts to any place worth going."

– Beverly Sills,

American opera singer

Training methods are designed to develop skills pertaining to stability, finesse, accuracy, striking strength, and sensitivity with the staff. Some training routines are intended for the advancement of a specific skill while others develop multiple abilities at the same time. The activities and exercises in this chapter will focus on the development of these skills as they were traditionally taught.

Hyun Gwan: Circling Staff

Hyun gwan (圈棍), or circling with the staff, trains staff stability, accuracy, and finesse for single-ended pole methods. In this exercise, the practitioner guides the staff around the circumference of a circular object for a set number of clockwise and counterclockwise revolutions. As the practitioner grows accustomed to the circumference of a particular apparatus, the training implement is replaced with a smaller adaptation to challenge the practitioner's level of proficiency. The beginner typically starts with a large rattan ring that hangs on a wall. Rattan rings with smaller circumferences, tea cups, and the heads of nails are the different circular measurements that are used to train this circling skill.

Steadiness with the staff leads to a greater sense of control with the weapon as it is wielded in training or in combat. As the practitioner trains to stay on the circumference of the circle, a feeling of stability with the staff is developed. The steadiness and control that are fostered by hyun gwan yield directional precision in techniques. As the individual grows accustomed to this practice, finesse is layered to this training sequence, adding another dimension to the group of skills that are cultivated. Finesse is an intangible classification that distinguishes a very good practitioner from an excellent one. It facilitates deflection, redirection, and disarming methods against an opponent – all actions that assist staff striking techniques.

Sa Baau: Sand Bag

Sa baau (沙包), literally sand bag, is an essential part of developing staff striking skills, strength training, and coordination. Sa baau training comes in a variety of forms ranging from oversized to handheld bags. The large bags train double-ended pole strikes while the smaller bags work on strengthening singe-ended staff techniques.

Daai sa baau (大沙包), the large sand bag, is typically the size of a hanging punching bag found in any fitness gym. The practitioner will strike the bag with double-ended pole techniques, alternating between left and right ends. While striking is one aspect of this training apparatus, understanding how to transfer integrated force effectively from the practitioner's body to the bag is the priority. It is important to recognize that the bag is dead weight compared to the liveliness of an actual opponent. Hence, solid staff strikes on the bag are merely preparatory exercises that will be customized to the dimensions and skill level of the opponent in actual combat.

Siu sa baau (小沙包), the small sand bag, is generally the size of the sand bag that is used to train tit sa jeung (鐵沙掌), or iron palm, in Chinese martial arts. The practitioner will wield the staff in a single-ended position, training lifting maneuvers with the pole. The bag provides resistance by weighing down the tip of the pole as the practitioner attempts to prop up the bag and strike it in mid-air. This drill trains the explosive force that is needed to initiate a technique and exercises the coordination to strike in the middle of executing a technique. As the practitioner becomes proficient in this particular training routine, striking accuracy is emphasized to raise the standard of practice.

Dim Faat: Point Method

Dim faat (點法), literally point method, refers to a series of exercises designed to develop accuracy with striking techniques. Hyun gwan, or circling the staff, trains circular motions while dim faat pursues point attacks – particularly vital points found on the opponent. The staff is handled in a single-ended manner, emphasizing the tip as the focus of integrated force. The object traditionally used to train point striking is the almond, or hang yan (杏仁). Initially, the practitioner places one almond on the ground and performs repetitions of the downward staff strike from a stationary position. The next stage requires the practitioner to stand one stride-length away from the almond so that the practitioner can train the step and strike method with the almond target. The stepping gradually increases to a three step strike, developing the practitioner's precision while in motion.

In the next phase of training dim faat, two rows of almonds are placed alongside the practitioner's path, obliging the individual to strike each almond while stepping forward in between the two rows. As the individual's agility and accuracy improves, a more challenging routine involving the random placement of almonds on the ground for the practitioner to strike is incorporated into the training regiment. The unpredictable nature of this arrangement is meant to mimic the spontaneity of combat.

In the final phase of training in this manner, almonds are placed on the ground as well as attached to the wall to train the precision of downward strikes in conjunction with forward thrusts. At the onset of this training method, the practitioner strikes in the sequence in which the techniques are arranged in the form. As progress is made, the practitioner smashes the almonds arbitrarily – again, simulating the heat of combat.

Muk Jong: The Wooden Post

The muk jong (木樁), literally wooden post, was simply a tree or wooden stump before it was customized with appendages to resemble the limbs of a human being on the muk yan jong (木人樁), or wooden person post. Originally, the branches on a relatively young tree acted as an opponent's limbs, and the practitioner would perform techniques around those parts in an effort to perfect the principles and purposes of those techniques. Today, many martial practitioners have adopted the use of the muk yan jong to support their training efforts.

Training with the wooden post develops the practitioner's skills in a number of different ways on a number of different levels. Firstly, both single-ended and double-ended staff methods can be trained on the muk jong. Aside from striking experience, this practice directly deals with range and the manner in which strikes can be maximized. Since double-ended staff techniques are suitable for close-quarter combat, the practitioner can gauge the best striking distance by analyzing the effectiveness of different strikes on the muk jong. Attacking methods that are too close are jammed or checked, and strikes which are just beyond the reach of double-ended strikes will miss or merely scrape the wooden post. This practice enables the practitioner to understand and grow accustomed to the distances in which double-ended pole methods excel. At the same time, single-ended staff techniques address the longer range, employing thrusting, ramming, and swinging strikes. While the distance is different for this manner of using the staff, a command of capitalizing upon the attributes of this single-ended approach is comparable to the double-ended pole experience – to ensure that the greatest result will materialize from the practitioner's maximized effort.

One of the fundamental tactics of staff techniques is to disarm an opponent. While stripping a weapon away from an opponent is the typical impression of disarming an adversary, to disable the opponent by splitting limbs and separating joints in order to prevent further attacks is the actual emphasis of disarming methods. This is practiced by maneuvering the tip of single-ended and double-ended pole movements around invented joints or limbs on the wooden post or tree. The circular, suppressing, and striking motions are critical components found in stripping techniques. Round motions are evasive or ensnaring actions; downward, upward, and oblique staff strokes are severing movements; and, thrusting, charging, and shattering staff methods attack vital cavities and pulse points on the practitioner's body. Although this may sound excessive or extreme, it is the nature of combat and a strategy to survive violent and unrelenting encounters.

In due course, practice on the muk jong integrates the experiences from the other training methods: hyun gwan, sa baau, and dim faat, elevating the practitioner's overall impression and understanding of skill while evolving the practitioner toward a sense of martial achievement.

Chaai Gwan: Paired Pole Practice

While apparatus training fosters the development of specific staff skills, chaai gwan (儕棍) – or partnered pole, is an essential aspect of learning the intricacies of the staff and the applications of its techniques with an actual person. Chaai gwan links personal skill with interpersonal interaction, enabling the practitioner to study the manner in which staff techniques can be effectively applied within the controlled setting of fixed routines that eventually lead to the exploration of freeform function.

Fixed routines are initially trained in stationary stances with dynamically-wielded staffs. The practitioner at this stage learns how to apply the first four of the eight staff forces, or baat ging: tiu, saat, seut, and jong. While lifting, suppressing, thrusting, and ramming forces, respectively, are issued by one practitioner, those same forces are trained to be equalized by the opposing partner. Both individuals are exposed to resistance training through actual contact as reaction skills are cultivated.

In the intermediate stage, the latter four forces of baat ging: paau, paak, sou, and hyun are exercised between partners. Raising, swerving, sweeping, and encircling motions are practiced in a manner that promotes the sensation and understanding of energy discharge and force dispersion. The energy exchange that takes place teaches the individuals to adhere and lead defensively, and to initiate and redirect offensively. It is the interaction of yin and yang – yielding and attacking, softening and strengthening, subsiding and energizing, that the practitioners learn to recognize at this juncture of chaai gwan. The practitioners begin to acquire a sense of finesse and refinement of technique, raising their levels of reaction to interaction while moving toward assertive intent in their actions.

During advanced paired practice, practitioners combine baat ging with baat faat, merging action with application under the pressures of simulated combat with a partner. Footwork is incorporated not only to address the importance of mobility, but also to regulate the proximity and range embedded within each staff technique. The appropriate proximity produces the ideal range that is required to infiltrate the opposition's dead gate. The footwork developed during this phase teaches the practitioner to maneuver into the opponent's sei mun in an observable and investigative manner. Such practice and experiences also tend to reduce the surprise of the unpredictable nature of fighting. With regard to staff ability, sensitivity and subtlety are cultivated. The practitioner is able to detect the slightest changes in an opponent's force, direction, or intent. In turn, this sense of sensitivity is used to encourage and inspire the practitioner to make his/her own movements imperceptible and invisible – ideally.

When all of these skills are achieved, the practitioner is well prepared for the uncertainties of actual combat.

Sudden situations will not overwhelm, and favorable conditions will not be underestimated. The chore of individualized training and the challenge of partnered practice are merely the means to enlighten the practitioner. The understanding that leads to knowledge, the determination that drives intent, the fortitude that fosters courage, and the passion that fuels commitment are the intangible facets that lead a practitioner to a mastery of the art. It is the harmonious union of skill and spirit that defines Kung Fu.

CHAPTER SEVEN

Practice & Praxis

"There are some things that you learn best in calm,

and some in a storm."

– Willa Cather,

American Author (1873-1947)

Among the traditional armaments of ancient China's rural and provincial areas, the staff was possibly the most accessible and readily available weapon. However, the knowledge to execute its techniques was not as easily attained from a master, and the wisdom to wield the weapon in a just manner rather than through sheer brutal behavior was equally absent.

Survivors from actual warfare and victorious individuals involved in securing the safety of their villages from marauders and roving bandits quickly learned from the uncertainties of combat the most effective ways to defend and the most efficient ways to kill. These warriors often became regarded as the sifu, or teacher, of a particular village and were responsible for the instruction of their knowledge and skill. It is from this tradition that Chinese martial arts were characteristically preserved.

Classical Instruction

As with any expert in any field, the secrets to a master's martial skills were highly sought after, fueling a sense of distrust and perpetuating a guarded perspective when it came to instruction. This was typically the culture of traditional Chinese martial arts. With regard to instruction pertaining to the pole, the sifu customarily taught in three modes: laan (攔; block), da (打; strike), and saat (殺; kill).

Blocking was trained first to establish a mindset of defense, enabling the master to assess the student on multiple levels which included talent and character. The fundamentals of blocking allowed the teacher to observe the progress of an individual. A student who could replicate a movement from sight was viewed as having potential and an inherent ability for the style while an individual who required in-depth instruction for movements was typically handed over to a senior student who would be able to walk the junior through the technique. The master's method in this case was to personally instruct the talented members so that they in turn would teach those who needed further instruction. Laan as a primer also enabled the teacher to evaluate the temperament of a student. An individual content with the pace of instruction would be considered a reverent and worthy student; however, an overly zealous practitioner could be perceived as having an agenda, capable of undermining the master's school. The instruction of blocking at the outset of learning within this circumstance was designed to temper antagonistic and aggressive attitudes.

When the student demonstrated an aptitude and the integrity to continue, the master moved onward to the instruction of striking methods with the staff. An understanding of defense facilitated the student's learning of sophisticated staff striking methods. While a staff could be used very crudely by anyone to beat, break, or bash in a random manner, a disciplined methodology gave rise to efficient skills that could be applied consistently and effectively. Blocking mannerisms performed flawlessly became striking techniques simultaneously if the practitioner was shown by the master. Additionally, advanced methods of parrying and deflection were actually tactics that led and lured the opponent into defenseless positions whereby more powerful attacks could be employed. Da was a stage of learning that distinguished a serious student from a casual trainee. Since the actions of the individual represented the character of the master, striking methods were imparted with a discerning eye. Those who could defend and attack proficiently maintained a high standard of excellence and were considered leading practitioners of the martial art.

In exceptional cases and circumstances, students selected to be the custodians of the system, or disciples, were shown the lethal methods of staff techniques. Saat was typically reserved for heirs to the system whom the master believed could handle the responsibility of such lethal knowledge. At this stage in the practitioner's learning, striking became the primary means of defense due to its effectiveness through the economy of action. Knowledge of lethal locations and the strategies to access them were transmitted from master to apprentice, typically to safeguard the system or to gain the advantage in times of warfare. This was typically a critical juncture for the apprentice. Such expertise required a virtuous nature to balance the potential for an abuse of such power. In many instances, masters withheld key elements from certain individuals even though they may have been elevated to the status of disciple. While this was a measure for the master to continually monitor the integrity of the disciple, it often served as the source of rifts and rivalries between the individuals. As a result, many lethal techniques under the designation of saat were never revealed or lost in the name of unworthiness.

The following example demonstrates the continuum of instruction from student to disciple and prevention to intervention to lethal application:

Yiu Fung Gwan: Waist Sealing Staff

Laan: Prevention – The practitioner blocks the frontal third of an opponent's attack to avoid being struck.

Da: Intervention – The practitioner simultaneously blocks an opponent's attack while striking the opponent's grip with the frontal third of the staff.

Saat: Lethal Application – The practitioner blocks an opponent's attack with the middle section of the staff while simultaneously striking the opponent's temple or eye with the tip of the staff. This is followed by an upward swing with the butt end of the pole, striking the right temple or neck.

The Transition from Training to Combat

Intense training will provide a practitioner with a set of skills over time, but it does not guarantee that the practitioner will be proficient in combat. As the individual moves from solo to paired practice, the training dynamic changes – just as the conditions change from prearranged sets and sparring to the unpredictable nature of actual combat. It is important to understand that the purpose of training is not only to prepare the individual for the unknown, but to reduce the shock of the unexpected.

On the physical level of training, practice must reflect the system's principles, and the principles must guide the individual's practice. However, the actions must correspond with an operational mindset in order to maximize the individual's overall achievement. A practical frame of mind raises the standard of individualized training and leads the practitioner closer to a level of confidence toward combat. To promote the proper mindset, the practitioner needs to be conscious of five particular factors as techniques are trained: mindfulness, visualization, intent, internalization, and extension.

Mindfulness is an acute awareness to the subtle movements of the staff, the slightest actions of oneself, and the significant details of the surroundings. Being attuned to each of these aspects enables a practitioner to understand the intricacies embedded within each technique. Visualization is an important strategy in perceiving and interpreting each movement. It provides the practitioner with both an image and idea of what the technique is expected to do. At the heart of all movements is intent which drives and directs techniques. Intent enables the practitioner to concentrate on a specific goal or target while acknowledging the seriousness of a situation and the severity of a technique. To internalize, in this context, is to acquire the skill of maneuvering the staff to such a degree that reactions are instinctive and responses are appropriate. Internalization gives rise to reflexive movements that are not merely automatic, but purposeful and suitable for the situation. Often an afterthought or even neglected concept, the extension or follow-through of a technique is critical to the effectiveness of its execution. Without follow-through, the technique fails to transfer the full force of the action and compromises the intent of the execution. When an individual trains in isolation, all of these essential elements must be observed prior to engaging in paired practice, otherwise, the techniques will have no purpose and the execution will have no effect.

During partnered training, both practitioners have the opportunity to learn and explore staff methods within a controlled setting. Making the change from solo practice to working with another person significantly raises the level of an individual's proficiency. However, it is important to understand that the key to any successful partnership is trust. Without this relationship, techniques can easily be misconstrued and escalate toward unwarranted violence, ultimately defeating the value and purpose of this manner of practice. Once this has been established, a different set of expectations and principles are necessary for each practitioner to fully benefit from this form of training. The five aims of partnered practice are: acclimation, comprehension, execution, examination, and exploration.

Partnered training initially enables an individual to interact with a live person within a martial context. This familiarity establishes a level of comfort and compatibility so that techniques can be trained safely and productively. During this stage of acclimation, the individual realizes that solitary training differs greatly from paired workouts. Furthermore, different partners yield different approaches – ability, size, speed, strength, and strategy all vary with the uniqueness of each individual which necessitates customized considerations during partnered training. Exposure to such experiences provides the practitioner with a well-rounded awareness to the varying degrees of conditions and situations that exist in physical confrontations. As the individual begins to observe and make note of the different scenarios that can arise, an understanding that techniques are multi-faceted begins to take hold. The practitioner begins to recognize concepts and principles that were initially introduced in theory but are now manifested in practice. The greater connections that are made between principles and practice, the more effective and efficient the execution of techniques should become. However, while this shapes the way that the practitioner will implement methods and maneuvers, there is a hidden hazard of overconfidence and complacency that the practitioner may face in this phase of partnership practice. During this critical juncture, motivation needs to be supplemented with an analytical and investigative attitude toward the performance of techniques. The practitioner needs to examine the training circumstances to ensure that maximized proficiency is aligned with the individual's unique attributes and personal limitations. This approach serves to foster growth rather than support stagnation. Ultimately, experimentation grounded within the system's principles will lead to personal mastery and universal understandings about the nature of confrontations.

When it comes to actual combat, the ability to switch modes from submission to survival will determine the success or failure of a hostile situation. Essentially, during partnered practice, there is a regard for safety; in combat, there is a regard for survival. It is important to note that the conditions that exist in prearranged drills or unstructured sparring still follow the mindset that the practitioner is in training and learning mode, *not* murdering mode. In the climate of training, practitioners operate out of a submission standpoint – the moment a technique or series of techniques has been performed by one individual, the other will react and respond often in the unspoken spirit of sportsmanship, which means that the session will end and restart at the point of capitulation avoiding unnecessary injury. In an antagonistic situation where a physical altercation is unavoidable, the individual must assume the mindset of a survivalist. In such violent scenarios, an attacker, or attackers, may be relentless, necessitating an equally self-protective determination on the individual's behalf. Such extreme instances warrant extreme responses, and it is in these moments where training reflexes must support survival instincts. A submissive attitude under such conditions can lead to dire consequences.

It is here that the practitioner must learn to prepare to deal with danger, and this needs to be trained. Traditionally in Pak Mei, one particular way that this readiness can actually be developed is to train one's sense of offensive defense. This means that the individual needs to think in terms of not just defending, but attacking to defend. This does not necessarily mean beating your opponent to the punch, although this can be a strategy. Offensive defense is an assertive approach in response to a hostile physical confrontation. For instance, rather than just stopping an opponent with a block, the block itself should actually hurt the opponent. While this should not necessarily be trained with a partner as a result of safety issues, it can be practiced on a training apparatus such as a customized wooden dummy. The practitioner will visualize an attack and respond in a simultaneously offensive manner. As this becomes ingrained and instinctive, the next challenge is to desensitize the body's sensory systems. In this phase of training, the practitioner is subjected to a variety of sense-inhibiting stressors. To hamper the senses of sight and smell, sticks of incense are burned below a practitioner while he/she trains with the training equipment. In this focus-building and fortitude-forming activity, the smoke acts as an irritant compelling the practitioner to attack the training apparatus in a forcible manner or to surrender to the lofty fumes. Another obstacle is the spontaneous banging of cymbals or pots by one's training partner to acclimate the practitioner to unexpected loud noises or screams during combat. These obstructions are done so that the practitioner's immediate emotional response in the face of a shocking situation will not overwhelm or impede the individual's ability to function.

Customarily, the Pak Mei practitioner's approach to a violent physical confrontation was to end matters – permanently. One of the precepts toward combat was: *Cheut sau bat lau ching, lau ching bat cheut sau* (出手不留情, 留情不出手) – *Should your hands have to go out, do not hold back your feelings or intent; if you hold back your feelings or intent, do not put out your hands.* While it may be quite easy to take this saying to an extreme, particularly during the period of China's Civil War between the Nationalists and the Communists in which founder Cheung Lai Chuen contributed his knowledge and skill in many ways to support the Nationalists, many legal consequences can result from such a way of thinking in today's civilized world. In the case of a fatal outcome, the martial artist in today's times must assume complete responsibility for all of his/her actions; and in a court of law, murder carries severe penalties, often regardless of a claim of self-defense, that can greatly alter a person's life in an unforeseen and unfortunate direction. It is always best to use caution and wisdom before succumbing to the more primal characteristics of rage and impulsiveness, particularly with martial knowledge and potentially lethal methods at one's disposal.

Learning to Balance Fire with Water

Intense training as described in the previous section needs to be properly balanced with guided meditation and an adherence to a strict moral code. Such esoteric practices yield unexplainable side-effects that can alter the chemistry of the brain which can lead to the irreversible impairment of the practitioner's body, mind, and spirit. Hence, the hormonal toxicity and flood of aggressive sensations that comes with such training needs to be tempered with the calming effects of qigong and the mantras of goodwill. Without these safeguards in place, an individual can pay a very heavy price for the cost of such severe training. The healing properties and reflective nature of qigong practice serve to metaphysically "cool" the excessive "fire" that is produced from intense mental and physical training with a "water-based" equalizer. Excessive fire can lead to the premature degeneration of the physical body and the untimely deterioration of one's mental faculties. This breakdown of the body can be averted by an in-depth understanding of the metaphysical properties of fire and water, constantly monitoring one's emotional stability and state of mind, and adhering to a steady schedule of qigong practice.

Many who pursue a study in traditional Chinese martial arts in modern times cite discipline, self-defense, or a unique pastime as primary reasons why they decided to partake in what would otherwise be considered a domain reserved more for military personnel than the average everyday citizen. Since the motivations of martial arts practitioners are varied and vast, safeguards must be established to prevent misguided decision-making and unwise choices from being made. As such, the Pak Mei creed was established by Master Cheung Lai Chuen to ensure that the proper etiquette and moral codes are followed by exponents of Pak Mei Kung Fu.

In general, poetic translations are approximations, at best. The rhythms, context, and multi-layered meanings in the native language can rarely be conveyed verbatim into the host language without encountering awkward phrasing issues or even non-existent equivalents. However, minor adjustments without major infractions toward the original content can provide a close and meaningful interpretation of the text, and in some instances, even enhance the translation into the host language.

The couplets in the Pak Mei creed are written from right to left and top to bottom in a mnemonic manner – a method that can be easily memorized and imprinted in the mind due to its rhythmic pattern. Even though it is said to have been passed down by the ancestors within the Pak Mei clan, the true origin of this code of ethics is unknown. What is most important is that a core set of guiding principles is in place to lead the practitioner on a morally correct and ethically sound martial journey.

白眉派祖傳訓詞

縱學無有萬相英學學專　白
然得親親兩逢雄得仁祖　眉
廢白有無黃不半功學專　派
石眉義義金是點夫義師　祖
作拳則不也忠莫能學專　傳
金與可可不良欺守功武　訓
磚棍傳教傳輩人己夫道　詞

Pak Mei Code of Martial Ethics and Conduct

According to the code of the creed, a Pak Mei practitioner must:

First, honor your ancestors.

Next, revere your teacher.

Then, concentrate on your martial arts.

First, learn humaneness.

Next, learn righteousness.

Then, learn Kung Fu.

After you have mastered Kung Fu,

You become empowered

And you can defend yourself well.

DO NOT:

Deceive,

Oppress,

Or take advantage of others.

Should you meet someone

Who is not

Loyal or virtuous,

You may not teach that person,

Even for 10,000 ounces of gold.

Even if someone is a relative,

If that person is not

Righteous or virtuous,

You may not teach that person.

However, if someone is

Righteous and has principles,

You may teach that person.

After you have learned

Pak Mei martial arts,

There is great value within you.

Anything that you come into contact with

Will reflect that value –

Even a stone.

These adages provide supervision toward honorable conduct, critical thinking, and good judgment. In the sphere of social dynamics and human interaction, it is important to understand the influence of proper etiquette and the ramifications of imprudent behavior. The Pak Mei creed advises the practitioner to exercise introspection and instinct to understand the extent of personal responsibility that one assumes when embracing the martial arts as a lifestyle.

It emphasizes the value of one's existence and defines one's place in the world.

About The Author

Williy Pang has over 30 years of interest and experience in Chinese martial arts with nearly 20 years dedicated to Pak Mei Kung Fu. Several of his articles focused on Pak Mei Kung Fu have been featured in *Kung Fu Tai Chi Magazine*.
He resides in New York City.